Dig DEIP in Dentistry

Dental Emotional Intelligence Proficiency

Lauran Star

Copyright © 2012 Lauran Star

All rights reserved.

ISBN-13:
978-1479360215

ISBN-10:
147936021X

A note from Lauran Star

Regardless of the market downturn, many dental practices are reinventing themselves from the inside out. Dental Emotional Intelligence (DEIP) will help you determine what your strengths are and how to improve upon them. While improving your DEIP you will also make yourself more marketable for the economic rebound.

This book is divided into six sections — the first is an overview of Emotional Intelligence and where Dental Emotional Intelligence fits in. The second through the fifth are focused on the specific development areas of DEIP. In each section, we examine the specific proficiency definition, what it looks like and how to improve. The tools are in your hands and it is up to you to put them into action.
Additional reading suggestions are available on my website at www.lauranstar.com

To your success!

Lauran Star

ACKNOWLEDGMENTS

The completion of this book would not be possible if not for the breadth of work and research done by Daniel Goleman, Laura Belsten Ph.D., Reuven Bar-On, and others who have dedicated their profession to enhancing the world through emotional intelligence.

Section I

DIG DEIP
Dental Emotional Intelligence Proficiency

What is Dental Emotional Intelligence Proficiency and why is it important?

When I tell dental practitioners that I am passionate about improving their Emotional Intelligence to increase their business, I am always entertained by the responses. This one is my favorite: "Well, some of my patients need Emotional Intelligence to help level off their mood swings and hormones."

DEIP has nothing to do with hormones, mood swings or true emotions! It has to do with how we handle ourselves in relation to others around us. It is a measure of how aware we are of ourselves in relation to others, in any environment. It is that simple.

Dental Emotional Intelligence Proficiency (DEIP)

DEIP is a form of knowledge that drives our success in work, life and our relationships. Research in this area has become quite popular. In these studies, dental practitioners who demonstrated high Emotional Intelligence had the following positive results:

- increase in patient/client retention
- higher rate of customer satisfaction and retention
- decrease in stress and positive job satisfaction
- less likely to be scrutinized regarding malpractice and had an overall reduction of practice risk management
- the ability to change and grow in any economic climate

Did you know that up to 80% of success comes from Emotional Intelligence? The rest is a direct result of your Intelligence Quotient, or IQ (Goleman, 1996).

Here is the great part of Dental Emotional Intelligence ... It can be learned!

So how does Dental Emotional Intelligence Proficiency (DEIP) fit in?

DEIP is a subset of Emotional Intelligence skill sets. Emotional Intelligence has over 24 competencies ranging from Empathy to Organizational Awareness. DEIP looks at the top 15-skill sets that top dental practitioners and dental schools focus on.

Let us face it, dental care is an area which patients tend to neglect due to a variety of reasons. In a recent poll, Dr. Ali (2010) uncovered the top five reasons patients "forget" to return six months later. Shocking, or not, the number one reason patients hate to return is due to the overall attitude of the staff and the dentist. The patient tends to feels lectured- to, they are ashamed of their poor habits, and the dental office itself is intimidating. Yet, when the economy goes down– dental care need is on the rise. More patients forgo the follow-up and only see their practitioner when there is an emergency, and we all know it may have been prevented.

DEIP is all about how we relate to the patient and others in the practice. It helps provide a safe and friendly environment where patient success thrives.

Many clients will ask - Do I have to be strong in all of the 15 skills areas?

No. You do not have to be strong in all 15; however, you should be aware of them. You also need to be mindful - DEIP is like a muscle. If you are strong in one area you need to continue to strengthen this area or it may weaken It also is important not to stress over all 16 skill areas. You can take the Social-Emotional Intelligence online assessment (available at www.lauranstar.com); you will discover your strengths and what areas need development. Select one strength, and one area of development or weakness to work through before moving on to other skills.

The DEIP Health:

Emotional states are funny little things, as they result in all kinds of hormonal changes in the body. One example is when we find ourselves angry, upset or stressed; the gut (stomach, large and small intestines) produces cortisol. That is not bad if you are in a fight or flight situation (such as a bear attacking you), however keep in mind that cortisol results in:

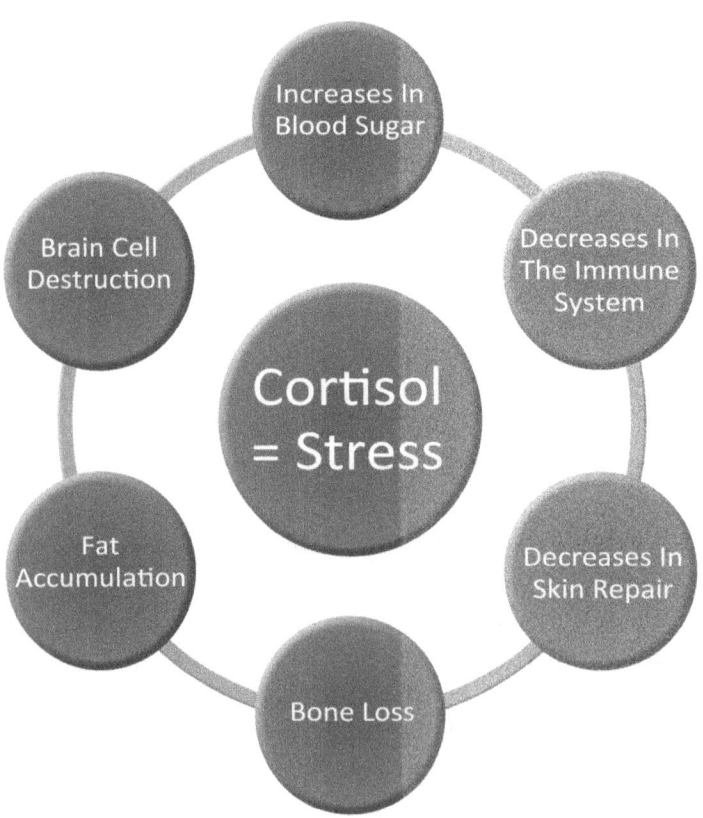

Another Example: The opposite also is true. If you are relatively stress free, calm and happy, the body/brain produces dehydroepiandrosterone (DHEA). DHEA is a natural steroid hormone the body produces. It is also the most abundant hormone in the body. DHEA has both positive and negative effects on aging, brain function, memory, cancer, and more. When DHEA is low (due to stress since cortisol attacks DHEA), the negative aspect of low DHEA is seen verses when in balance or high levels the positive is seen. So if you are stressed, the results of low DHEA equals your aging process speeds up. *Just think of all the wrinkles you will save by understanding your DEIP.*

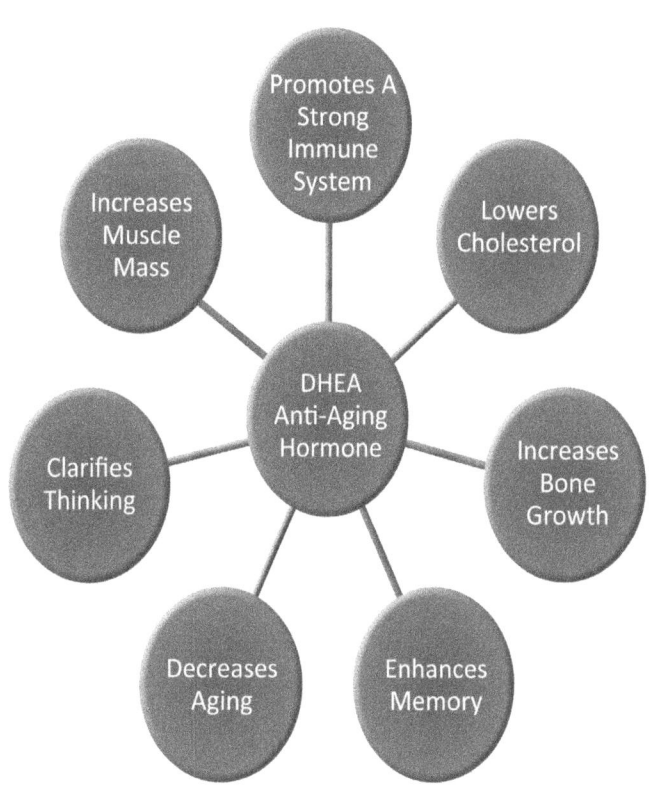

Awareness of your LEIP is the first step in ongoing development.

Here is what DEIP looks like:

Self Awareness - Your awareness of your own emotional state	Other Awareness - Your awareness of others
• Self Awareness • Personal Empowerment	• Empathy • Business Awareness • Service Orientation
Self Management - How you behave	Relationship Management - How you manage your relationships
• Self Control • Integrity • Proactive Action • Drive • Resilience	• Developing/Mentoring Others • Communication • Influence • Visionary Leadership • Trust

Coaching is the single best method to improve Emotional Intelligence!
(Goleman, 1996)

What is coaching?

Coaching is a personal and professional methodology that enhances your strengths to achieve your goals. As a result, work and home life will be improved.

Coaching is a relatively new field and tends to be more action-based rather than diagnosis-based. A coach does not presume to have all of the answers. Instead, they serve as a thinking partner to create a synergistic or co-creative relationship with their client.

While working with a professionally trained coach to discover your innermost desires, you co-create a plan of action that will help you reach your goals faster and more easily than you would have on your own.

Research about coaching tells us

- coaching is recognized as a proven way to improve dental practice performance
- dental practitioners involved in coaching found an overall improvement in their work/life balance
- those who were coached had a better understanding of how to approach gender decisions and issues
- dental practitioners who were coached created a better relationship with their peers, direct supervisors and more importantly their patients
- those who were coached exceeded their personal and professional goals

How do you find a coach?

Coaches should be specialized and their training should reflect their specialty. A client can find coaches specializing in Intrapersonal Relationships, Life Goals or Career Transition. Remember that as a prospective client, you must first define what YOUR needs are.

Coaches that specialize in executive, leadership and business coaching typically are at a Master's Degree level or beyond. They also tend to focus in one area or another (example healthcare, dental care, finances) versus being broadly focused.

Life Coaches typically have coaching training and enhanced life experience and may fall anywhere on the educational continuum. Typical life coaching focuses on relationships, networking, weight loss and so forth.

It is important that your coach be a certified (and active) member of a coaching governing body such as The International Coaching Federation (ICF) (www.coachfederation.org/). This organization requires that members adhere to high ethical and educational standards and be committed to ongoing training. Certification requires that continuous educational credit hours be earned every other year.

You can locate a coach via the International Coaching Federation at www.coachfederation.org/find-a-coach or contact Lauran Star at Lauran@Lauranstar.com for a referral or complimentary session.

For more information on coaching, read, *"No Winner Got There Without a Coach"* – contact Lauran Star for your copy at www.lauranstar.com.

Lauran Star

Section 2

Self Awareness

Welcome to self-awareness. This is development Area 1. In this section, we have self- awareness and personal empowerment. As you probably guessed from the title, this is all about you and your own level of awareness and empowerment. It has little or nothing to do with others. This is where you gain the crucial level of self. Understanding your awareness and power level allows you to work on how that relationship embraces others.

Here is the kicker of self awareness — once you have an awareness of self, all other development areas (2, 3 and 4), become a little stronger.

Self Awareness - Your awareness of your own emotional state • **Self Awareness** • **Personal Empowerment**	Other Awareness - Your awareness of others • Empathy • Business Awareness • Service Orientation
Self Management - How you behave • Self Control • Integrity • Proactive Action • Drive • Resilience	Relationship Management - How you manage your relationships • Developing/ Mentoring Others • Communication • Influence • Visionary Leadership • Trust

Self Awareness

Self- awareness is the ability to understand why we react the way we do in every situation. It also encompasses the skill of regulating the subsequent reactions of a situation to achieve the best results. Self awareness is the first step in improving DEIP, it all starts here!

This is THE most important DEIP skill set. No matter how strong we may be in this area, we need to keep working on it. We all have blind spots. If self awareness is lacking, then the rest of the competencies and our perception of the daily situations will be off balance.

A note of self awareness denial: If you feel you have strength in all the areas of the competencies listed on the prior pages, you may be in "development denial" regarding self awareness. Consider the following example: Have you ever worked with a practitioner who thought he/she was an outstanding communicator, when in all actuality you felt he/she struggled to get her point across in a meeting or with a patient? The practitioner in this case has a strong self awareness, however it is false.

In the dental field, self awareness can be seen among not just the practitioners but also in patients.

Here is what it looks like:

- Knows the "what and why" about their feelings. They understand what is driving the emotional/gut response and act accordingly.
- They are always in control of their emotional side and understand the full ramifications of their actions.

Example: They understand the outcome if they are late to work regardless of traffic. Patients will be waiting and thus the whole morning schedule will be thrown off–so they plan accordingly.

- Depending on the patients' and staff's needs, they are aware of themselves in alternative situations and adjust their behavior accordingly.

Example: With some patients you can enjoy fun behavior whereas other patients are all business. My husband is an engineer–thus "just the facts" suffices, whereas me who tends to be a bit more social so "more fun, please".

- Utilize their insights when a situation is causing havoc on their system, to seek solutions and to gain strength.

We have all worked with a practitioner or patient who just cannot seem to get over his/her "stuff" in life. They are lacking the emotional bandwidth to reign-in their feelings and/or life is all about them. They are difficult to work on and with – thus your role is to have enough DEIP to either say something to them or overlook it.

When we interact with a professional who is strong in this area, we are drawn to them because they give us positive energy. The opposite is also true. In creating your own self awareness, you also create an awareness of other interactions taking place. This will help you assess situations down the road, as well as give you an idea of how to improve.

Therefore, before we move on to the Tips section, keep in mind there are two great ways to improve self awareness: (1) hire a coach and (2) journal!

A word on Daily Journaling:

- Journaling consists of you writing about you — how you feel, situations that went well, situations that went poorly, what makes you special, what your dreams are, where you wish to be in the future, goals and more. It is all about you.
- Be honest with yourself, and open yourself up to your fears and concerns. What keeps you up at night? Write it down — and you will fall back to sleep rather than wasting energy on the issue.
- Journaling is personal; share it only if you wish to share it.
- Find a quiet moment. You do not need an hour, if you have five minutes, write away. Create a five-minute window, which can be a coffee break or wine break depending on the time of day.
- By writing this down — you purge it from your brain so you can reflect, embrace and grow later.
- Embrace yourself and what you write. All that you are makes you who you are, and that is pretty amazing!

Reflect on what you wrote, a day or two later. This will provide you with solutions as well as insights into your behavior and situations.

Tips

Journal ...journal and then journal some more. It only takes a few minutes to write down a thought or an emotion. Utilize the journal flow sheet attached.

Journal Flow Sheet:

The Empowered Journal has a custom format that includes this flow sheet. Please visit www.lauranstar.com more information and to get your own.

Situation	Emotional State	Why/Cause	Positive or Negative and Why	Your Response	How to Improve ACTION
What took place	What did you feel	The reason	How did it affect you	Response	What should you have done

Become aware of how YOU react to stress. Is it physical? For example, your shoulders tighten, your jaw clenches, and you get a headache or your heart rate increases. Is it emotional, presenting as yelling, crying, screaming or withdrawal? Then identify how you would like to react. This will give you a target behavior goal.

When you feel stressed, do a body check. Stress causes body issues you may not even be aware of; therefore your body is like a stress beacon for you. Ask yourself... Are your shoulders tight, teeth clenched? Are you biting your lips? Do you have a headache? Ask yourself why you feel this way. Note what is causing the emotion — Are you stressed, frustrated, angry, and impatient? Then write it down! This will remind you when you clench your teeth you are actually stressed out, and then you can identify the stressor.

Take is a step further and empower your patient – how do they react to stress. While they are in the chair are they relaxed? Are their hands clenched? Ask how they are feeling today – headache, stomach pains. Create a patient check in list of symptoms – it will help you gauge their comfort in the practice.

By empowering your patients to take action – you strengthen your own skill set!

Body Check:

Headache_____

Stomach Pains_____

Twitchy Eyelids_____

Rapid Breathing_____

Heart Palpitations_____

Sweaty Palms_____

Heavy Perspiration _____

Ringing in Ears _____

Pain Behind the Eyes _____

Do an emotional self check throughout the day. How am I feeling right NOW? Note it and journal it!

Finally, get to the nitty-gritty. Ask yourself, "Why am I feeling _____ and what can I do to change the behavior?"

In all of the above tips, ask yourself "How would you like to respond… What action would you change…?"

In awareness comes clarity and growth.

Personal Empowerment

This is the ability to get what you desire in a tactful way. It is the overall ability to assert yourself in any situation and then maneuver the situation into a win/win resolution for all involved. It also is visible and viscera, a strong, inner calm. It is the inner belief that you are in charge of your life and can accomplish anything you want, if you want it badly enough. It also is the ability to let go of those things you cannot control or wish not to control.

In dentistry, we can see Personal Empowerment both in a practice as well as in the practitioner. It is more than the outward appearance of both, as it is that internal calm, that all is right and as it should be. Patients tend to trust an empowered practice and its staff more easily than if the practice is lacking personal empowerment. This is not to be confused with confidence – as too much confidence can turn potential patients away.

Here is what it looks like:

- You know it when you see it: This practitioner or office has it all going on. They know what they want and get it. The practice has a clear brand – or has a reputation that matches its strength. They tend to be cutting- edge.
- This practitioner is in control of his/her life; they do not believe in fate as they are in charge of their own success!
- They dream big and achieve those dreams.
- Accountable is more than a goal to the practice. It is a verb- and is done daily, all the while not taking themselves too seriously.
- Practitioners reach out to others freely and offer support and mentoring.

From a practice standpoint, the practice has a positive flow to it. Chaos is not a standard of care especially in emergency situations.

Amazingly, those with personal empowerment tend to attract others with personal empowerment both in business and in life.

In business and in play I love working with empowered people, as they are continually empowering those around them without even knowing they are doing it. Think of people in your life who make you feel energized after seeing them. These are the friends who say … "Let's go white water rafting;" and then follow up, bringing the fun to fruition, regardless if they had ever done it before.

Tips

Create a list of personal boundaries. If you are the "go-to person" for everything in the office – every decision – every action – find and empower others to take those tasks off your plate. Create a list of tasks such as, purchasing, order entry, dealing with sales representatives, marketing, billing, market awareness, networking, etc. Assign someone else to be the point person. You are empowering that person to take a more active role while empowering yourself to stay focused on your own tasks.

This is the same if you work too many hours, which results in seeing your family less – set a schedule you can stick to and let others know about it. Carry this list with you.

Find a mentor who will help you gain confidence and keep you accountable. This can be a coach or colleague. Do not choose someone you are overly close to, like a mate/spouse, as you will want to push back when this person challenges you, and you may ask them to define exactly what you did or did not do. Mentoring another colleague also helps to keep you in tune with technology and market changes.

Create a list of things YOU excel at and things YOU have accomplished. Then keep it with you for times when you are feeling like you have failed. It is amazing how often we see others strengths, however forget our own. This is a nice reminder. You can add this to your journal.

My Rock Star List:

_____
_____
_____
_____
_____
_____
_____
_____

Network. Find a friend or colleague who is strong in this proficiency; observe their energy and their commitment to their own life. Let them know you are borrowing some of their empowerment and model after them.

Journal. Yes once again, journal when you notice your own empowerment level is high and when it is low. Identify the cause, and find a solution (take action) to improve.

Find a theme song! That's right; choose a song that reminds you how strong you really are! It may sound crazy however, I use "Happy Girl" by Martina McBride, when I am sad, and I use "The Warrior" by Patty Smyth, when I am going into a stressful meeting.

When you feel victorious after a tough composite or a difficult cleaning patient, celebrate with your theme song and a victory dance. Feel free to create a theme song list for your individual situations.

My Theme Songs:

Situation	*Song:*
Down in the dumps	"Happy Girl" by M. McBride
Stressful meeting	"The Warrior" by P. Smyth
Celebrate	"FireFly" by Katy Perry

Put it to work; once you have strong personal empowerment help others discover their own. Take a leadership and/or mentoring role at work and help empower those around you. In doing so you will continue to build your own personal power muscle ... use it or lose it.

Lauran Star

Section 3

Others Awareness

Much like self awareness, others awareness is all about you and how aware you are of others and the immediate environment you are playing/working in. Great practitioners have this development area nailed; they know how and what others are feeling, all while having their finger on the surrounding pulse of the practice.

Self Awareness - Your awareness of your own emotional state	Other Awareness - Your awareness of others
• Self Awareness • Personal Empowerment	• Empathy • Business Awareness • Service Orientation
Self Management - How you behave	Relationship Management - How you manage your relationships
• Self Control • Integrity • Proactive Action • Drive • Resilience	• Developing/ Mentoring Others • Communication • Influence • Visionary Leadership • Trust

Empathy

This proficiency is the ability to understand and relate to another situation or cause. It is the ability to share an emotion or understand where the emotion is coming from, then help process that emotion. One with strong empathy also manages her own level of empathy so it does not impede the overall performance of a job or of life.

Empathy is NOT sympathy – as empathy is to place yourself in another's shoes.

Women tend to have a higher empathy base than men however, empathy is not a given strength. It takes energy to produce empathy, therefore this proficiency needs to constantly be strengthened and toned.

In dentistry, pain and fear is often associated with the word Dentist regardless of age. Both the practice and the staff need empathy. As a practitioner ask yourself:

Is your waiting room sterile or patient friendly? Is it appropriate to your audience – if you treat both adult and children do you have reading material for both – or is the office brand (reputation or feeling) set more toward one patient than the other?

How are the exam rooms set up – do your patients see the tools of the trade as they sit down? How does this calm them?

The office staff – are they friendly, neat and open? Is the staff a role model for the patient as far as oral care goes? Are they approachable or standoffish?

Here is what it looks like:

- Compassionate and understanding, when outside issues interfere with another's ability, all the while maintaining control of the situation. They keep the job's tasks in mind.

Example: Are you focused on the patient or the phone that is ringing down the hall that no one is answering?

- When you are having a bad day, this is the person who you turn to as he/she can separate out the emotional conflict from the tangible conflict, and understands how to work through the situation.
- They understand their patient's fear and concerns and can calm them easily. They just psychologically "get" their patients.
- The ability to place yourself in the other persons shoes.

Empathy is a key component to approachability in the dental field. Studies have demonstrated this proficiency is lacking among dental practitioners and may increase the resistance or decrease retention among patients.

Think about this – who do you see for your own dental treatment and why.

Empathy is a HUGE MUST have. So if you are low in this proficiency remember you can increase it with a bit of help.

"Happiness is your dentist telling you it won't hurt and then having him catch his hand in the drill." ~Johnny Carson

Tips

Get in touch with your own emotions. Review your emotional state and note how you are feeling and what the cause and action of that feeling is. Becoming aware of your own self will help you understand others.

Listen to what is being said, and monitor body language. Look for the external clues that will give you internal perception as to where a peer truly is emotionally. Clenched hands are a dead giveaway of stress and fear.

Don't be afraid to openly, one on one, identify what you think you are hearing or seeing. Validation is a powerful tool! It is not enough to be empathetic; you must share that with the person for whom you are feeling empathy. It is o.k. to openly understand the fear of being in the chair with your patient. It lets your patient know you are in the moment with them.

Practice taking on another perspective. The old saying, "Walk in my shoes," is a great way to increase empathy. Open yourself up to another person's situation and explore the emotional effects. Remember when a patient sits in your chair they are bringing along the days worth of stress with them. Sometimes having them just breath and relax will get them in the right mindset.

"Sounds like," is a great opening line when identifying hidden emotions. Rephrase statements while looking for a deeper meaning.

Don't overdo it or try too hard. Believe it or not, empathy will come naturally once you allow yourself to openly accept the emotion behind the message.

Body Language. Identify what body language means — if you struggle with learning body language, read *The Power of Body Language* by Tonya Reiman.

Business Awareness

This is the understanding of how the dental business and the market space function and perform, along with its abilities, potential and results. This proficiency is imperative for survival in the dental field–as many new practices are springing up daily.

It is the understand that the field of dentistry exists within a social economic system that feeds off each other.

Business Awareness is critical for any planned change process. It is gaining a better perspective of the practices mission, market awareness and power awareness allies. Think of this as "Business Intuition."

Practice Mission (brand)	Market Awareness	Power Awareness (allies)

Practice Mission:
This is as simple as asking yourself ... what do you want the practice to be known for? It goes beyond the practice implication as each practitioner has the opportunity to sub-brand – What does he/she wish to be known for. It is more than just stating your mission – you must then act on your mission. If you do not want to work in the pediatric market – then don't. Make no exceptions. If your focus is on oral health – be sure your office screams it – tweet about oral health issues, have downloaded articles in the waiting room, be sure all the staff (including the front desk) know the mission and can help build the mission.

Example:
The office I go to for general dentistry is a restorative and cosmetic dental practice. Their overall goal (mission) is complete oral health. My dentist has a very high level of DEIP – he also is remarkable with his work! He is true to his mission – as the focus is on restorative and oral health and he spends a great deal of time helping his patients take their oral health to the next level.

His staff also has their own missions – one hygienist's mission is on oral health, but is also known for being straight forward and not allowing excuses (ok so I don't floss every day ... and yes I do confess). She also is up to date on all oral health issues and shares with her clients. Let's just say while some hygienists go for a walk during their breaks – mine is on the web reading hygiene and oral health articles – and this drove me to her.

The practice mission is more than what your place on your website. It is a set of core values beyond the 'brand' the practice embraces daily.

Market Awareness:

This is an area in which some practitioners may fall short. The understanding of what the market will pay ... what you can offer... and what is accepted... is crucial in a dental practice. It is knowing that how much is billable based not just on materials but also time output and thus charging the "right" amount. Market awareness is a ten-mile radius surrounding your office space. Ten sounds low however, data supports patients typically will not go beyond the ten-mile marker for routine dental or medical care.

I have seen some practices where whitening is "given away" – not by choice. They undercharge in a market where the going rate is twice what they charge. So what ... well as much as I hate to admit it ... cost comes with a perceived value – charge low the value is low, charge too much the value is too high. Perceived value also goes on to note the lower the value the less compliance. Thus, we must find a happy medium. To do that YOU must know what the market awareness will pay.

This is not only the case with whitening – I have seen it with crown work, root canals, orthodontics and more.

More to the point – if you are looking to open a pediatric practice in an area where four already exist, you need to ask yourself:

- What will I offer that is different?
- Why should patients switch over to my practice?
- Can the market space provide the number of patients I need to substantiate business?
- What power awareness do I have and what is at play?
- What social networks are your patients on? How can you engage them there?

Power Awareness

It is as it sounds ... and a bit more. To understand you need to ask yourself

- What are the power plays in your market?
- Is there an alliance formed or in place before you open a new practice?
- Who is in your inner circle for referrals?
- Who is out of the circle and can they do damage?
- What tools are at your disposal to increase your power awareness (i.e. Twitter, Facebook, media, etc)

Successful dental practices are all about power awareness regardless of the type of dentistry being performed.

Imagine an Orthodontic practice that relies heavily on word of mouth *versus* a practice that relies on word of mouth plus their power alliances – for referrals. Who do you think has more patients?

Networking is building power awareness as it builds allies. It keeps you tuned into what the market space will spend, who is doing what in your space, who is doing damage to your alliances, and what tools work.

The key to all of this is the sweet spot – where all three intersect. This is where you build your practice

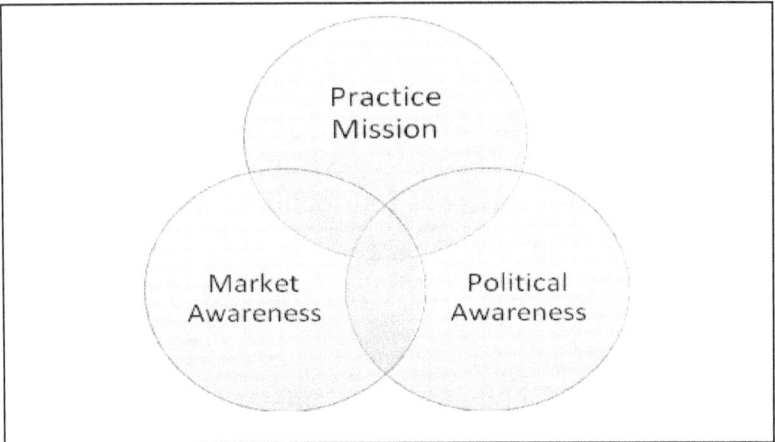

Here is what it looks like:
- Understand what power struggles, social networks, and political relationships are at play in any given situation and within the current market space.
- Take the above further by making the networks and relationships work for the practice.
- Accurately read situations or external forces and realign them with the department or practice mission.
- Encourage individual mission statements from the whole team.
- Be knowledgeable with what is happening in the market before the market exposes itself. Know the next big thing and act on it.

- Understand and utilize those around you who can help further your mission – i.e. other dental practices, distributor representatives, sales representatives and staff.

Example:

Think of whitening – launched in the late 80's some offices jumped right on the band wagon as they saw profits as well as improved patient oral health. In the 1990's, magazines were beginning to focus on the whiter smile – there was research being done around the topic of the younger smile equating to attitude and confidence. In the new millennium whitening is a common procedure – you can even purchase it at the local store for in-home use. Studies show the benefits beyond whiter teeth and the media is all over it – you can get a better job if your teeth are white (according to some).

Yet I can think of several offices that still do not offer whitening...

In the dental field, technology is rapidly changing. One can either thumb their nose at technology or embrace it. They can remain in the 1970's (including the shag rug) or modernize and keep up with chemistry. Here is the kicker – whatever your choice, patients and colleagues know it and they tell everyone.

Tips

Understand where the practice struggles. Where does the practice fall under practice mission/ political and market awareness. From there create a plan of action addressing that specific arena. Seek outside help if needed.

Dental Club : Keep up to date on the latest technology, not just procedure based, include hygiene, office administration, latest trends. Have each person in the practice be empowered as the "go to person" for a topic. Invite other offices to join you – meaning if you are a General Practice office, invite a Pediatric, Orthodontic, Prosthetic and Endodontic office to join you quarterly to share what all have learned. Look at the network of referrals you just established!

Uncover allies that have a pulse on the market and mentor with them. Ask them how they gain their information. Participate in an information swap, as it is an agreeable practice. This is an exchange of information as well as the building of an alliance within the corporate structure, that will prove beneficial down the road.

Watch the political powers at work. Awareness is a key skill set. Be aware of the changes or interplays you see happening when you're at work and note them.

Create a Market Awareness sheet: This is a working document and should include:

- Who practices in the surrounding 10 miles from your practice
- What are their specialties
- What is their brand – what are they known for
- What does the current market space bear for pricing on certain procedure
- What is the age population in the 10 miles around your practice
- Gender of population as well as ethnic considerations
- Who is in your network – is it working – if not why
- Who or what are the outlying dental offices that just do not "fit" the market space

This information may be as easy to get as a phone call or asking the next person who comes into the office. It also will help you establish whom you are marketing to and with what.

Business awareness is not only left to the practice owner as it is also imperative the team of practitioners also embrace the awareness. In doing so the overall awareness of the practice increases. Share the mission with your patients'. Ask for feedback as patients are a wonderful resource.

Service Orientation

Service Orientation is the ability to listen to and understand the customer as well as anticipating customer needs. The focus is to provide the highest level in customer satisfaction to everyone.

In dentistry, service orientation is a cornerstone of daily business. The saying , "Do unto others as you would have done to you", is not enough in business . What determines good service is a perception of the customer.

While being courteous falls under this proficiency it also requires accountability for action follow through. This proficiency is one of the easier and faster ones to work on however, it is more than just being nice. Listening and communication skills are required.

An office strong in service orientation will also find they have a high retention rate as well as patient referral for new business.

Here is what it looks like:

- The patient is the focal point for whom ever is working with him/her – it is all about them, not you.
- Understand and ask questions to determine the persons needs and then again to ensure the persons needs were met.
- Listen carefully and empathize with the persons concerns or fears.
- Offer relevant information on new technology as well as procedure outcomes.

Tips

Learn to listen to what your patients are asking, look for the deeper issue. As practitioners we need to remember many of our patients come to the office with fear, therefore we need to be sure it is the true concern we are hearing rather than a masked one.

Empower yourself to think outside the box when it comes to customer service. What can you do differently that other offices are not doing?

Remember to thank and **reward loyal clients**.

Ensure service orientation is part of all **employee's performance plan**. Improving awareness is necessary.

Reminders: post reminders throughout the office.

Survey your patients and staff yearly, if no issues continue however after one bad review re- do the survey three months later and seek improvement. Be sure to ask:

- What do you like about the practice?
- If there was one thing you could change in the practice what would it be?
- How can we better serve you?
- How does the waiting room make you feel?
- How do you perceive your overall oral health?
- What would you like to see us offer in the practice?
- How do you perceive the following and their values?
    - Whitening
    - Product sales
    - Oral hygiene
    - Endodontic treatment

Ask, what did your patient like in the office from which they came from. We all have dental history, why rebuild the wheel. Ask all new patients what they loved about their old practice – and then borrow the tip.

Section 4

Self Management

This section focuses on how you behave in situations. It is all about you.

Self Awareness - Your awareness of your own emotional state	Other Awareness - Your awareness of others
• Self Awareness • Personal Empowerment	• Empathy • Business Awareness • Service Orientation
Self Management - How you behave • **Self Control** • **Integrity** • **Proactive Action** • **Drive** • **Resilience**	Relationship Management - How you manage your relationships • Developing/ Mentoring Others • Communication • Influence • Visionary Leadership • Trust

Self Control

Self control is the ability to control your reactions and responses to situations as well as your behavior style. It is the ability to moderate your impulses, leaning more towards the positive rather than the negative.

Self control is vital proficiency in any business and personal transaction. We all know someone in our midst that lacks this proficiency; they have a hard time curbing their need to one-up each other, voice their opinions at the wrong time or with the wrong tone, have an emotional outlet at the wrong moment, etc.

Lacking this proficiency can call into question integrity, honesty, professionalism and approachability.

Here is what it looks like:
- Stay calm under stress and pressure. Composure is their middle name.
- Ability to regulate and process your actions, communications and emotions — allowing these out at the appropriate time.
- Think clearly regardless of the situation.
- Solid grasp on the bigger organizational picture/market picture and keeps it in mind when stress or turbulent changes are present.

Tips

Self awareness is the first step in gaining self-control is (you guessed it): journal, journal, journal! Identify what situations are causing you to lose self control, and then discover what the trigger is. Once this is noted, you can calmly define how you would like to respond to this trigger.

Trigger Chart

Situation

Deep scaling with a difficult patient

Trigger	**Reaction**	**New Action**
constant complaining	Demand Attention and move forward	Empathize not sympathize

Identify a thinking partner—someone who is unbiased and has solid self control, and model after this person. Ask her/him how they are keeping their composure in the toughest situations. Create a list of tips from this person.

Create a list of triggers. This will come from journaling; now keep a separate list of triggers, your reaction as it is now, and the reaction you desire. By keeping this list you can review your triggers and the behaviors you desire before stressful situations..

Give yourself a totem of control. If you know you are going into a dicey situation, remind yourself you are in control. Create a totem and bring it with you. No, I am not talking the survivor "stay on the island" totem. I have a very smooth rock that was given to me years ago; I keep this in my pocket when I am at work, in meetings or when stressful situations arise. By holding the rock I am reminded ... I am a rock of control.

What is your totem of CONTROL?

Mirror, Mirror. Coaching is a good tool for self-control issues; however, we see things after they happen. That being said, find a peer that can hold a proverbial mirror up to you—showing and identifying where control was lost. Also try to understand what others are feeling when control is lost or what is the result of the lost control.

Learn to deep breathe. We all think we know how to take a deep breath, amazingly, we forget when we are stressed or emotional. So follow these five easy steps, and the more you practice the more it will become a habit.

> 1. *Find your quiet place. This can be anywhere as long as you are comfortable.*
> 2. *SLOWLY breathe in through your nose, expanding your abdominal muscles while inhaling.*
> 3. *Now hold your breath for 3 seconds... One one-thousand-... two one-thousand.-... three one-thousand.*
> 4. *Slowly exhale out your mouth. This need not be a quiet exhale; it may be beneficial to hear the air leave your body, thus clearing your mind and body of any negativity and stress.*
> 5. *REPEAT. Deep breathe three or four times.*

I take several deep breaths before a stressful meeting, while in traffic, when I have a headache, or when I am nervous before doing a presentation or speaking engagement.

Find more "me" time and relax. Exercise with yoga or Tai Chi, take art classes, or listen to soothing music.

Integrity

Integrity is simply doing the right thing in the workplace based on your values as well as the organization's values. Hopefully, both you and your employers are in sync; if you are not, there will be conflict. Integrity is doing what you say you will do and is within your value system. Ethics and integrity go hand in hand. It is made up of honesty, truthfulness, principals and management of expectations.

This is the competency that everyone thinks they have and yet, when we ask a co-worker, friend, classmate, or peer, we find some of us may need a competency booster shot.

Imagine if you worked in an office where the goal/ mission statement was overall oral healthcare and yet the office staff had poor oral care. As a hygienist, does your mouth sparkle without bad breath when you are discussing oral care with your patient? How about whitening – do you sell whitening in your office while employees need to whiten? If you're an orthodontist are your teeth straight?

These are physical examples – let's dig deeper – If you promise to provide the best treatment today's dentistry can offer ... are you truly providing what is promised or what is affordable – and is there a difference in your eyes. Are you staying up to date on new technologies? Can you differentiate between 'new' verses improved?

Here is what it looks like:

- Acts ethically, or always does the right thing.
- "Go-to person" for advice, as they are honest to the core.
- Knows their core values and sticks to them even in conflict.
- Lives their life within their own value and belief system.
- Keeps commitments, so you can confidently plan your time with them.

- Manages the end expectations, never overpromising or overstating the end results.

Believe it or not, integrity is a learned behavior verses a biological one. Integrity is a behavior that can be built upon. Integrity grows as we mature, as we learn from past mistakes, from ourselves as well as others.

Tips

Create a list of values you feel strongly about. Place them in an area you view daily, like your journal.

> **My Values**
> *Be open and honest with everyone I interact with.*
> *My belief is the following ...*
> *TRUST is a key to success.*
> *I will not tolerate ...*
> *I will always strive to do the right thing!*
> **The ideal work environment looks like ...**

Post this list where you and others can see it. It is a constant reminder of your values as well as a blinking light for co-workers and patients.

Use a phrase that forces you to tell the truth such as, "I must say …" or "The right thing to do is …" or "I believe …."

Review situations where your principals were in conflict, examine how you reacted and the end result. **Ask yourself "How did I feel afterwards**?" Note this in your journal as it will reinforce identification and positive behavior for the next time.

Consistently implement the three tips above; make them a habit, not a hobby.

If you find your core values are in conflict with your employers, you may need to adjust your employers or employment. Openly discuss the situation with a coach, mentor or trusted friend to co-create a solution.

Proactive Action

This is acting in advance or foreseeing future challenges and heading them off now rather than later. It is taking action to control a situation or outcome. Proactive action involves being motivated to be ready for any situation. It is the ability to seize control and create opportunities.

Proactive action has been coined as "motivation, proactive awareness and persistence," however, proactive action is a bit deeper than that definition. We all know this person in our lives—they see issues well before the rest and make action changes that alter the outcome.

In the dental world, technology is rapidly changing. The only way to stay ahead of the curve is awareness – market and technology awareness. It is not enough to "buy" based on one persons word anymore – we need to do a bit more research to ensure what we are buying is in fact the best technological advancement that your office needs. Sounds difficult right … however with the internet and a few keystrokes it is not.

Here is what it looks like:
- The ability to create opportunities for yourself as well as your practice, and then do it.
- Up to date on their job tasks, technology and market awareness.
- "Procrastinate" is not in their vocabulary – their actions occur before one can ask.
- It is not just a salary, it's the full adventure.
- Can see the end goal, on a larger picture, and therefore is driven toward optimal success.

Tips

Positive is as positive does. Stay positive when facing challenging tasks, and look for unique solutions.

Give yourself permission to think outside the box. All too often it is our fear of failure that keeps us in the box or from reaching out with a new idea. Remember it is ok to fail as long as you learned from it. Take the initiative to start new dental programs within the office.

> *"There are no failures - just experiences and your reactions to them."* T. Kraus

Think in terms of the Big Picture and What If's
When you are handed a new project, brainstorm by yourself or with another employee and ask, "What could possibly go wrong with this? What could go right? And how can it be better?" Next, create solutions that address the issues and discuss how the project could be better. Make a list and then take them higher up to hash out.

What Could Go Wrong
- A
- B
- C

What Could Go Right
- A
- B
- C

What Could Be Improved
- A
- B
- C

Solutions
- A
- B
- C

Working with your journal can help you master proactive action.

Write about what holds you back in your position, what you struggle with, and where you would like to go. Then address each item, brainstorming new ideas. Have fun with this and be creative.

I have been fortunate enough to see how proactive action can thrive in the dental world. Kathleen, a clinical coordinator for a large family dental practice, decided years ago to create a group of female dental practitioners who meet monthly to discuss anything and everything in the dental field. This group started small with only seven members, however it now – less than two years later- has over one hundred members, ranging from pediatric to orthodontic. The group is comprised of coordinators, hygienists and Dentists all coming together to share.

Just think for a moment how much is learned in one meeting regarding technology, procedures, billing options, latest research, market data and patient referrals.

Drive

I once asked a dentist what his drive was. His response was, "A Toyota Sienna."

Drive is goal-setting and then achieving those goals. It is going above and beyond for you and your organization's success. It is the desire to be the best you can be while realizing your own limitations. Drive is the inner strength you have to complete tasks and goals. It is the motivation to get what you want, or to complete the tasks at hand.

Drive is a learnable behavior. Some seem to be born with it while others have to work at it, however it is a muscle, and like all muscles, it must be used keep it. Yes, you can lose your drive. Complacency is the number one killer of passion and motivation in ones job satisfaction and performance. This is one reason we must flex our drive muscle.

Drive is also a habit and thus we need to create a drive habit to go down the road. It take at least fifteen solid goal-setting and achievement actions to make drive a habit.

This is what it looks like:

- Always is striving to exceed new goals.
- Higher standard of excellence than others, does more and goes above and beyond.
- Constantly trying to improve oneself with more education, classes, techniques, etc.
- Calculated risk-taker.
- Accountable for all they do.
- Goal setting and achievement is a habit.

Tips

Find a partner that will hold you accountable, and then set goals that stretch yourself. Make them specific and doable. Be sure this is someone who can hold a mirror to you and show where goals are falling short.

Example: This year the practice will grow by 20% in new patient referrals.

Define what excellence means to you. All too often we are unclear as to what excellence looks like and then what it means to our lives. Define what excellence looks like for you and then how it improves your life.

Example: Excellence means outstanding client relationships, and that means more referral business, more money, less time spent marketing and more time with family.

Forecast where you want to be in five years and assess whether you are on track. If not, figure out how to get there. If you get stuck consider hiring a coach or finding a mentor to help you.

Question yourself regularly about your performance. "Why did I—or why did I not—go the extra mile on this project or patient?" You might find out some very interesting things about yourself. Maybe you are in the wrong job or you saw inherent issues with the task at hand that prohibited success. The collected information can be positive, since employers hate wasting time on tasks that may have hidden or unresolved issues.

Create stretch goals for your future.

Make the goals SMART: Specific, Measurable, Achievable, Realistic and Timed. Then check them monthly. Post those goals where you will see them every day ... like in your journal.

These goals can be both professional and personal.

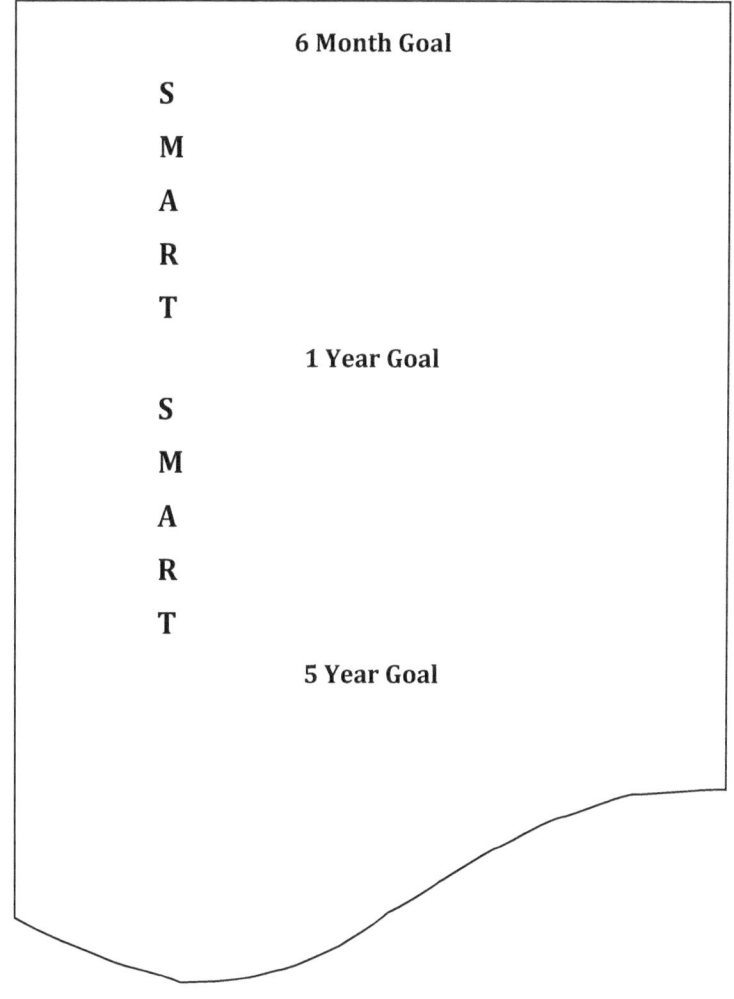

Resilience

Resilience is the ability to change, adapt and improve with the times. It is the ability to see an issue and its solution using a positive dynamic. It is the bounce-back factor. It is being empowered about the end results regardless of what the situation is. It also is being realistic and optimistic about the future.

In today's economic market, it is more important than ever to be resilient in your work and life. So many things are changing, and at such a fast pace! If you are not resilient, you may be left behind. Many dental practices are now focused on finding employees and partners that have this proficiency. The result is a greater positive atmosphere even during times of economic malaise.

This is what it looks like:

- Great coping skills and can bounce right back from challenges.
- Loves changes and challenges, and sees them as opportunities for growth.
- Flexible and adaptable no matter the situation.
- Rises above setbacks and then make them work for them.
- Makes lemonade out of lemons.

I recently had a client who was terminated from her employment for unknown reasons. She had worked with her employer for several years as a senior hygienist and earned an above-average salary. Her first reaction- shock, her second reaction was "what the heck, I never have been fired before; what should I do now?" She was somber as she thought through the whys ... and quickly discovered the *whys* matter, but not as much as the *now's*. Her action steps were as follows: she put aside the termination and began to identify and clarify what her skills were, she also explored what her core values were and how they fit into her career. From there she created a list of questions to ask the next potential practice to ensure a good fit with her skills and values. After the evaluation stage (one to two days), she proactively sought out employment with practices that fit her expertise.

She now states it was the best thing to ever happen to her; she grew and became an even better hygienist and team member through that experience. She bounced back faster and with more pep in her step due to her resilience.

Tips

Stop the negative self talk. When you say, "What was I thinking…? Am I good enough? I don't deserve … " answer your own question. Challenge yourself to change.

Surround yourself with people who are resilient and ask for their help or awareness. Many times we are not even aware that we are in failure or non-resilient mode.

Create a support system. Make a list of people who are resilient and can be your support system when you falter. List their characteristics.

When you suffer a setback, create a list of steps to take to get out of it. If you are stuck, then ask—ask-ask for help from your more resilient friends and co-workers. Brainstorm success.

Yes, I am going to suggest another theme song … like Chumbawamba's "Tubthumping" ("I get knocked down, but I get up again/You're never gonna keep me down") or Tom Petty's "I Won't Back Down." Download the song to your desktop, iPod and cell phone. You may be surprised how quickly this will make you smile, and help you bounce back.

Bounce back. No one is asking you to be 'Little Mary Sunshine', however do not be doom-gloom either. Find your balance and bounce back. You will waste less time and gain more energy.

Q-TIP, Quit **T**aking **I**t **P**ersonally. Sometimes bad things just happen, whether in work, home or life. Remember, decisions are not always about you. Assess the situation and see where you fit, or don't fit, in the grand scheme of the decision process, then take corrective action when needed.

Oh Yes ... Journal!

Section 5

Relationship Management

In this section, we will be focusing on how you manage your relations with others. It is about both you and your reactions to them.

Self Awareness - Your awareness of your own emotional state • Self Awareness • Personal Empowerment	Other Awareness - Your awareness of others • Empathy • Business Awareness • Service Orientation
Self Management - How you behave • Self Control • Integrity • Proactive Action • Drive • Resilience	**Relationship Management - How you manage your relationships** • **Developing/ Mentoring Others** • **Communication** • **Influence** • **Visionary Leadership** • **Trust**

Developing Others

This is the ability to foresee and understand what the development needs of your team or peers are, and then the ability to put an action plan together that addresses these needs. The development may be for personal growth or business growth, and also can fall under various categories. The end goal is growth.

Dental practices are built upon its employees' strengths. One must be able to see where strengths lie as well as where there are opportunities for development. A great leader and/or business owner will continuously evaluate his/her staff, seeking signs of weakness or development and noting strengths. This leader will empower his/her employees by training them to ensure their continued success and can utilize other employee strengths to the practices benefit.

An employer who does not re-invest in his/her team will find employee and patient retention as well as market awareness failing. The end result is declining revenue and increased cost to train new employees.

This is what looks like:

- Intuitive skills to understand where peers and staff are going, and then creating a plan of action to compliment the employee strengths.
- Interested in helping others improve and goes out of their way to ensure opportunities for growth are available.
- They mentors others.
- Is an avid learner that passes along skills learned.
- Provides timely and appropriate feedback with the end result in mind, while looking at another's development for improvement or enhancement.

Developing others is a great way to give back to all those who helped you in the past. In the dental field, tomorrow's practitioners are learning from today's examples, so why not mentor? When you develop others, you may find they can take on increased responsibilities, providing you with more time to focus on other tasks.

Tips

Take the time to know your peers and staff. Routinely ask what their goals are in work and life and see how you can help them achieve them.

Create portfolios of your staff, noting goals, drive, skills, areas of development and progress. Keep tract of upcoming due dates for CPR, recertification, CCEU's.

> *"Everyone has an invisible sign hanging from their neck saying, 'Make me feel important.' Never forget this message when working with people."*
>
> \- Mary Kay Ash

Create **employee performance management systems that include development and training.** Add a section to the quarterly reviews, which summarizes what was developed this quarter and what will be tasked for development for next quarter. This can be a simple document and shows you care.

Be part of their solution for growth. Make yourself available monthly to sit down and assess where the employees' or teams development is heading.

Look for or create opportunities for your employees. If you have an employee who wishes to communicate better, find a training class, create a communication role (such as an inter-office newsletter), or find a mentor for them to follow.

Celebrate developing others. When a milestone has been achieved by an employee or team—celebrate! This also will help create more awareness around your own desire to develop your people.

Team build! The practice is a machine caring for people–is it well oiled or rusted? Do the staff member anticipate each other's needs? Do they communicate with each other effectively?

"Everyone wants to be appreciated, so if you appreciate someone, don't keep it a secret."
— Mary Kay Ash

Influence

Having influence means having the ability to change or shift daily events. To effect or alter the events or outcomes through direct or indirect action. Influence is a combination of skills including: communication, negotiation, self control, integrity, organizational awareness and personal power.

Influence is one of the harder DEIP skills to learn, in part because influence has many facets that include, social networking, visionary leadership, self awareness and communications skills. It is more than just being able to effect outcomes, it is the ability to change others perception of issues while maintaining a balance on one's own integrity.

Not sounding simple is it... In dentistry, Influence happens every hour every day. Part of your role is to influence your patients to achieve solid and positive oral care. Influence is **then effected** by the patients' demographics. If you are treating a nine year-old one would have to use a different tactic to influence them to brush and floss twice a day as you would a thirty-two year old.

Demographics also come into play when trying to influence a patient to go with a root canal versus a tooth extraction – as finances may come into play as well as what the community "norm" is.

It is imperative a practitioner understands how the patient's demographics come into play and then can empathize with this demographic. From there, strong communication skills are required.

The same is said when we apply influence into the group practice where as one is trying to shift a policy or oral program to benefit the practice. Market awareness factors in alongside tact and communication.

This is what it looks like:

- Negotiates win/win situations because you are in tune with your peers and clients.
- Has the right support at the right time for the right campaign.
- Understands the power struggles within the organization and has created a team of supporters.
- Influence is felt even when you are not in the room.
- Change is your favorite word as you embrace and can rally the troops around it.

As you can see, influence is followed by team support – as you cannot have one without the other and creating change won't happen without influence. You probably can list several individuals who can get things done and several who cannot.

Here is the best part of influence- *those who cannot influence today can influence tomorrow, with a little help.*

Tips

Create a list of those who you know have this skill set. Now list their skills. With most DEIP proficiencies- awareness is the first step to gaining strength. Now look to see where you need a bit of tweaking and tweak.

Name	Skill Set
Maria	Strong Listener Empathetic Strong Leadership Skills

Define situations by goals, end goals and identify the players. Begin to network with the major players and understand their view on the situation. Create a plan of action—looking at the pros and cons of the situation versus the end goal.

Alliances-Create work place alliances with like minded individuals. Include teammates that have a degree of influence of their own.

Brainstorm with a few others. This must be an open assembly where no one is judged and everyone can speak freely. Brainstorm on skills, situations and tasks for influencing others.

Take risks. That's right, take a risk on a new opportunity. Take the lead role and uncover your personal power, organizational awareness, integrity, communication and negotiation skills. Do not be afraid to ask for help!

Look for opportunities where you have allies, situations where you can effectively influence others, and then put some of your new skills to use.

Communication

Communication is the ability to pass along information in a manner that is clearly understood by the audience. It is presented through verbal, written, tone, inflection and body skills. Sounds easy, right? Wrong!

This is probably the trickiest area for women and men, as tone and inflection are part of communication. Because men and women communicate very differently, the message can be confusing or even become lost. Let's face it, no matter the gender, some folks do not have a clue about how to communicate effectively.

It is easy enough to misunderstand an in-person communication. Now that email communication has become so prevalent, the potential for misinterpretation and harm is so much greater. Texting, blogging and tweeting are other forms of communication all with a different subset of rules and vocabulary (As if English does not have enough rules.)

Here's what it looks like:

- Listens deeply and without prejudice, truly hearing what the other person is saying.
- Eliminates or adjusts all emotions in their communication when appropriate.
- Takes notes when others are speaking and then clarifies what has been said.
- Remembers it is business and not personal. Q-TIP, takes criticism and feedback in stride, and does not take it personally.

- Writes and speaks in a clear and concise manner that is effective and easy to follow.
- Uses proper grammar protocols and checks for spelling errors.

All too often, communication is the first perception other individuals have about you. Consider the following: Did you speak poorly, with improper tone, or were you too loud? Did you listen to the conversation or interrupt with your own points? Were you yelling in the last email you sent? Did you spell correctly and use proper grammar? Were your arms crossed—closing out everyone? Did you roll your eyes? Are you aware you rolled your eyes? etc.

In job searching, grammar issues are the fastest way for your resume to find the garbage. If your email communications contain too many emotions (not facts) such as explanation points, hearsay, and emotional identifiers such as, (made me mad, can you believe, what was he thinking), it is the fastest way to become an irrelevant source, or to lack credibility.

Remember your body language is just as important as what you say. Standing with your arms crossed and frowning is the quickest way to be avoided at a party or business meeting, yet we do it all the time without even being aware we are doing it.

Keeping in mind the gender of your patient – as men like the facts and women like the story- will go a long way.

Tips

If you know you are a poor listener, keep a notebook with you when you are having a lengthy conversation with your co-workers or patients. Write down what appears to be important, and then ask for clarification at the end. **"So, if I heard you correctly, you need x, y and z, is that correct?"**

Listening skills are a learned behavior. Listening is like a muscle—you must listen, think, and then respond. All too often we think first, then listen and respond—yet what are we responding to tends not to be the true issue communicated. Try to take notes when the person is speaking, instead of processing what has been said.

If you know you are going to be presenting information, or even writing an email, create an outline of the points you wish to make, group them by category and bring this with you. Another example would be to use an email template. This also is a great way to format letters, or proposals.

Tape yourself. Bring a small tape recorder and ask everyone present if they mind if you tape the cleaning/procedure or meeting . Then listen to it 4 to 6 hours later, and write down what you hear. See if it matches what you were trying to convey.

Tone is critical in using email communications. Unless it's an emergency, never CAPITALIZE all letters. Readers can interpret this as yelling, as it draws rapid attention to the word- and stops the reading process. Please take care to spell correctly, and utilize proper vocabulary. Once it is written, and sent... you cannot take it back-thus the impression you are sending is one that will stick. Keep your tones soft, with proper inflections, thus keeping the interest of your listeners.

Take a communication class. If you do a lot of presenting, look at Toastmasters, a local training organization focused on public speaking. If you need help with grammar, hire a communication coach or look at the local community college for classes or workshops, or in my case hire a rock star editor.

Keep positive: If you know a meeting may be challenging, stay positive and think of the best outcomes. This will keep your tone neutral, and the conversation on track. Write down the upside or tone you wish to keep during the meeting on a sheet of paper and keep it where you can see it.

Visionary Leadership

Visionary leadership involves taking in the larger picture to move the practice or group to the next level by bringing the decision-making process to the forefront. These leaders are inspiring, innovative and agents of change, creating strategic plans for a better tomorrow. The key to visionary leadership is maintaining the big picture and offering compelling motivation to move others in that direction.

"Leadership is not who you are ... it is something you do and become"

LA Murabito

You know who this person is, as they see and think big and can back their vision up with a plan. Visionary Leadership stems from the individual and flows through the practice. Think of this proficiency as the thought leader in dentistry- always trying something new to create improved patient outcomes.

This is what it looks like:

- Motivated, compelling and inspiring when discussing a vision for the practice or themselves. You also know they will achieve their vision.
- Tactfully challenges the status quo, when it does not align with their vision.
- Creates a common goal and purpose for the team.
- You feel like you belong to something bigger when you are with this person.
- Inspires you to achieve more.

I will admit this is my favorite proficiency as those with visionary leadership are inspiring, amazing and fun to be with. They see the big picture and tend to be positive, motivating and trend setters. Their practices are ahead of the business curve. The best part of this proficiency, no matter what your role is in the practice ... you can be a visionary leader. Think of Kathleen, example used in proactive action. She had the leadership needed to get her women's group of dental practitioners off the ground. She also had the vision and determination to ensure the results – shared ideas – was met.

Tips

Ask yourself: What does visionary leadership look like, who has it and with what skill do they present it?

Decide **what your personal vision is**, what is it you wish to accomplish in the next five years, and think BIG. Be as clear and focused about the end result—it is not enough to say "I wish to be successful." Allow yourself to dream.

Now, **break it** down to chewable-size pieces. What are the action steps you need to take to embrace visionary leadership?

Find your passionate voice. What are your emotional values and how do they tie into your vision or your organizational vision? Put them together.

Now do this on the organizational level.

Find fresh perspectives on old issues- take an old issue and brainstorm big—anything and everything. Write it down and begin to see new breakthrough ideas.

Trust

Trust is having a firm reliance on the integrity, ability and ethics of a person or thing

Practitioners who are lacking in trust can damage not only the practice but also the field of dentistry. They undermine what the practice and its leadership stands for. Trust is not earned overnight, yet a lifetime of trust can be destroyed in 30 seconds or less. Trust must be earned as it is rarely given away.

"Trust is like a vase ... once it's broken; though you can fix it, the vase will never be same again." –Anonymous

In dentistry, we are already behind the eight ball when it comes to trust – as many fear or hate going to the dentist. You do not cause this ... however somewhere in everyone's memory is a painful dental experience. Generation X and beyond did not have painless dentistry as a child. Technology was not there yet. You have to ask ... Does pain equate to trust? No, however pain does equate to aversion and thus trust is critical to overcoming this obstacle.

Trust goes hand in hand with integrity and ethics with a strong dash of honesty. If it is going to hurt... say so. If you cannot make my smile perfect ... tell me. If there is an alternative procedure that is cost effective ... inform me. And when there is a curve thrown at me due to unforeseeable aspects of my teeth... empathize with me. However, never bullshit me.

In the dental field, trust goes along way and will win you many referrals if your patients trust you. It is important you understand how your patients view you and your practice. The reverse is also true – a lack in trust will cost you patients as well as your reputation.

Example: I trust my dental practice as a patient extensively – if my dentist says I need a root canal ... I need one. When he refers me to a specialist – I do not question it– it is where I go. I rely on my dentist to provide me with the best care possible. It took a year to reach this point – where, I felt my dentist was fully invested in my care. I refer everyone I know to his office with great pride and pleasure.

This is what it looks like:

- An open person who shares information about themselves.
- Transparency is their middle name.
- Honest and acts with integrity.
  Great follow-through on projects/tasks and commitments.
- Their goals are in alignment with their personal values
- Gossip is a six letter word – they just do not use.

Tips

It is OK to be wrong, just own up to it and make corrections. Admitting you are wrong builds trust.

Define what trust looks like. Keep this list handy so that when you are in a sticky situation you have a trust list.

Do what you say—always! If you find this hard to do then do not commit to anything unless you know 100% that you can.

Don't lie ever, and if you do, correct the situation.

Don't gossip. Always remember when you gossip you destroy trust.

Be open and honest regarding the details of a situation. All too often it becomes easy to embellish upon a situation.

Remember the truth will come out eventually—and embellishment hurts your trust factor.

If you do not have the answer just say so. You cannot know everything. Answer, "I do not know right now, however I will find out for you," and then do it.

I know it sounds easy to build trust however, this proficiency is often taken for granted. We stop 'working' on it because we believe we are solid here – yet on occasion we may slip. Those slips, if not corrected will cost you patients and reputation.

Section 6

Parting Words

Lauran Star

Take a moment and think about someone you look up to, someone you admire. What is it about them that draws you to them?

Surprisingly or not IQ is not even in the top ten as to reasons you were drawn to them. It is their emotional intelligence quotient (gentle, charismatic, passionate, driven, direct, professional ect.) or results from it.

You now have in your hands a tool that can help you increase your DEIP. What you do with it is your choice. DEIP increases as we become older, naturally, based upon what we have learned, modeled after and embraced. DEIP lessons can be both positive and negative. Improving your DEIP is a choice, not an accident.

It is up to you—you are in control of Your DEIP so dig in.

Please feel free to contact me if you have any questions, are looking for a DEIP coach or just wish to share your thoughts.

Best Wishes on your Journey!

Lauran Star

Lauran Star

Reference and Sources

Adler, N. (2006). Coaching Executives: Women Succeeding Globally. Coaching for leadership: The practice of leadership coaching from the world's greatest coaches (2nd ed.) (pp. 237-244). San Diego, CA US: Pfeiffer & Company

Belsten, L. (2006). Coaching Emotional Intelligence: The Art and Science of Accelerating the Achievements of Your Clients. CO; Boulder: Learnmore Communications Inc.

Brown, W., Bryant, S. & Reilly, M. (2006). Does Emotional Intelligence - as measured by the EQI - influence transformational leadership and/or desirable outcomes? Leadership & Organization Development *Journal, 27(5),* 330-351.

Cooper, K and Sawaf, A (1996). Executive EQ: Emotional Intelligence in Leadership and Organizations. NYNY: Berkley Publishing Group.
Cummings & Worley, (2009). Organizational Development and Change. Mason, OH: South-Western Cengage Learning

Goleman, D. (2006). Working with Emotional Intelligence. NYNY: Bantam Dell

Goleman, D., Boyatzis, R., McKee, A. (2002) Primal Leadership: Realizing the Power of Emotional Intelligence. Boston, MA: Harvard Business School Press.

Kotter, J., (1996). *Leading change.* Boston; MA., Harvard Business School Press.

Palmer, I., Dunford, R., Akin, G., (2009). Managing organizational change, a multiple perspective approach. New York, New York; McGraw- Hill Inc

Star, L (2010). LEIP Forward! Gaining Emotional Intelligence: Tools for Today's Woman Leader. Boston; MA.: Sweet Dreams Publishing

Star, L(2010). Emotional Intelligence Journal. Boston; MA.: Sweet Dreams Publishing

Reiman, T (2007*). The Power of Body Language.* New York: Simon & Schuster, Inc.

ABOUT THE AUTHOR

Lauran Star:

Lauran Star resides in New Hampshire where she enjoys a reputation among her peers and clients for offering integrity, the highest level of confidentiality and unflinching support, as well as candor and actionable solutions. Her focus is in the Medical/ Dental arena as well as Women's Emotional Intelligence.

She also served her country for ten years, as a proud member of the United States Armed Forces.

Lauran's academic background includes a Masters Degree in Industrial/Organizational Psychology from Argosy University and a Bachelors degree in Psychology from the University of Massachusetts.

You can reach Lauran Star at Lauran@lauaranstar.com

www.ingramcontent.com/pod-product-compliance
Lightning Source LLC
Chambersburg PA
CBHW061515180526
45171CB00001B/196